NIXES MATE REVIEW

ISSUE 24/25 SUMMER/FALL 2022

Nixes Mate Publications
Allston, Masssachusetts

All works copyrighted by their authors, 2022.

Book design by Michael 'd'Entremont' McInnis.
Cover image used with permission.

All rights reserved. This book or any portion thereof may not be reproduced or used in any manner whatsoever without the express written permission of the publisher except for the use of brief quotations in a book review or scholarly journal.

Philip Borenstein ·Publisher Emeritus

Michael McInnis ·Editor + Designer

Annie Elezabeth Pluto · Editor + Director

Hannah Larrabee · Guest Editor

ISBN 978-1-949279-44-3

Nixes Mate Publications
POBox 1179
Allston, MA 02134
nixesmate.pub

Dedicated to the memory of Gene Barry.

Gene Barry, a legend in the international poetry community, touched the lives of many, many people, myself included. He welcomed me into Blackwater Poetry group on Facebook, and we later became friends. In the pre-COVID world, I had the honour to read with Gene at the Červená Barva Press Studio in August 2017. And at Nixes Mate Books we were proud to publish his collection *Flaking the Rope* in 2018 and have Gene return to Boston to host his book launch at the Trident Booksellers Café. Gene was larger than life – a captain of language – a spinner of tales – a healer – a man of enormous talents – a man with a huge heart. He will be missed. May his memory live forever.

— Anne Elezabeth Pluto

Table of Contents

"It is a most hideous Article in the Heap of Guilt lying on you that an Horrible *Murder* is charged upon you; There is a cry of *Blood* going up to Heaven against you." — Cotton Mather

"I shan't own myself Guilty of any Murder, — Our Captain and his Mate used us Barbarously. We poor Men can't have Justice done us. There is nothing said to our Commanders, let them never so much abuse us, and use us like Dogs. But the poor Sailors" — William Fly

Mather, Cotton. *The Vial Poured Out Upon the SEA*. Boston: T. Fleet, 1726. Database: *America's Historical Imprints*, Readex/Newsbank.

"On Tuesday, the 12th Instant, about 3 p.m. were executed for Piracy, Murder, etc., three of the Condemned Persons mentioned in our Last viz. William Fly, Capt., Samuel Cole, Quarter-Master, and Henry Greenville . . . Fly behaved himself very unbecoming even to the last, to the hangman said he, 'You do not know your trade.' Their Bodies were carried in a Boat to a small Island calle'd Nick's-Mate, about 2 Leagues from the town, where the above said Fly was hung up in Irons, as a spectacle for the warning of others, especially sea-faring men; the other Two were buried there." — *The Boston News-Letter*, July 7-14, 1726.

DON MITCHELL

in a state of REM

Dreams are like touching texture

Fantasy, in vivid silhouette

        struts down the runway of your

            gorgeous, unconscious mind.

I am blissfully blind

Long enough to see

        everything.

              I shall take

a picture

before i wake,

        and see the light of day

             nearsighted.

MARTHA KAPLAN

If & When

If I loved you in blue filament
Stars would thread slowly, slowly in silver air

When silence moves like a great white shark
Mars bends to kiss the earth

If hope became the wind rushing across the plains
Coyotes would howl sea foam

When the red wolf bristles fire
Ice cries steel spears

If you swam naked in a yellow sea
White clouds would drip oil

When the hyena roosts in the baobab
Leopards stalk the sky

If hatred became a wild crane flying through the trees
Stones would sprout legs and run

LINDA LAMENZA

Splashdown.

Reentry wreaks havoc on the vestibular system. — nasa.gov, August 2020

As Bob Behnken and Doug Hurley float in the Gulf
and Mission Control entertains phrases like
nominal trunk separation
and nosecone closure,
my sister texts
It ain't summer til
you have space and hurricanes.

My brother texts
Just did a quick calculation:
at 17,000 mph if the astronauts
were traveling from Boston
to California, it would take 11 minutes.

Perhaps Bob uttered to Doug,
Did our wives even miss us?
Confided to each other
misgivings about the return to Earth.
Chaos, human hatred,
germs, reality television.
I can't tear my eyes
away.

SARA EPSTEIN

The Speed of Dark

Sam asks me:

"Mom, you know the speed of light,
Well, what is the speed of dark?"

Meanwhile, Nora's busy in the sandbox.
I had sent her outside to get some fresh air before going to Hebrew school.
She was mad that she'd have to go without her best friend today.
We look out the window to see her writing something in the sand,
  using the green, tall leaves from the lilies that border the sandbox to form letters.
I send Sam out to investigate, which he does, at the speed of light.
He comes back, serious, but with a gleam in his eyes.
"Mom, I think you need to go out there."
I go at medium speed.

"Mom," says Nora when she sees me.
"See the grave I'm making?
I'm digging so I can go in.
See what it says?" I do.
It says, "Here lies victim of Hebrew school, Nora D."

In the sand she has also written,
discreetly in lines not outlined in green,
but just lines in the sand, "Hebrew school sucks."
She tells me later she wiped out the "sucks" part,
so the neighbors wouldn't think poorly of her,
and keep her away from playing with their young daughters.

HADLEY DION

Roanoke

Your dad steals spotlight with a story,
he once rescued an owl from midnight
road. But when he awoke, the bird had exploded
with maggot insides.
I love the way
your family erupts, I yell
and become honorary member.

Dishes are washed and
beds are warm, we sneak
egg nog and cinnamon
whiskey. Binge watch a show you want to share,
turn down the volume on sex scenes. Prone to hiding
like little girls, wearing our early twenties
as makeshift
costumes.

In the morning, we walk along river
trail, where the community has been
ravaged by bath salts. Among heavy
pause, we find everything we need
in muddy puddle. Capture our reflections
in disposable camera. Cut the trek short
so you can pee in a coffee shop where they welcome
your name.

We buy a James Taylor cassette, belt out Fire
and Rain, drive through your favorite streets,
inhaling the houses lit in holiday
apparel. I am so lost but you know every road
like a sister.

Power Lines

MEGAN WILDHOOD

My sister believed her house burned to the ground. She wasn't the one to let me know she was safe – I didn't even know there was a fire. My mom, who had not replied to my last text four days earlier about my aunt's COVID battle sent a simple *K + L had to evacuate their home just now.*

Oh no! I dutifully responded. *Did K go pick up B? Where are they now?*
I f I wanted to know anything about my family, I had to ask the right questions. It's been that way since the dawn of time.
Not sure. They were headed to M's house. We don't really have room for them here.

For twelve hours, I struggled to breathe through spikes of mourning for our family baby grand piano that, if I had gotten my life together like every other adult does by their mid-30s, would have been safe and sound in the hypothetical happy home I should be living in with a husband I met in high school and everything else that my sister but not me has. I hated piano lessons, as did my siblings, and I never got very good, but I'm the only one who played the damn thing as an adult. My dad, who jokes that musical talent skips a generation in our family, has confirmed that this piano, which his late mother bought in the '40s, was mine. Also that I'm basically Grandma Jane reincarnate – which my dad but not me believes in. A therapist once inquired if my father fought a lot with his mother. That I knew the answer without having to cook up the right question said more to the therapist than the answer itself. (I'll give you three guesses about that and the hint that it starts with a Y.)

For the half day my family "just knew" that the fires I grew up hearing about on the news finally claimed everything one of us owns, I only cared about my piano. My sister may have lost everything but the clothes on her back, her 10-month-old, her husband, and their cat that L ran back for after they got the word to evacuate. And all I cared about was the piano.

Actually, the monster in me whispered, *you want everything your little sister has to burn to unrecognizable ash*. She, who may not be a monster but certainly had never tried as hard as I have to follow the rules, be a nice person, take care of everyone but herself, has *everything*. Everything I've been aflame with fear that I'd never get. Fear that my mom was right about why: who I am – too intense, too reactive, too sensitive, too *much*. I have been tangling with this monster for decades and it has hoped for some pretty gnarly things, some of which a therapist might gently suggest are germinations of jealousy. But that my sister lose everything just because she's not even trying to be a nice person? That's a first.

The Marshall Fire, the worst fire in Colorado's history, started December 30, 2021, burned for five hours and ultimately consumed just under 1,000 homes (my sister's ended up not being one of them) and all of downtown Superior. Hurricane-force winds spread the blaze fast throughout Superior and Louisville. Of *course* my sister lived in *Superior*. We – I say that like it's an 'all in this together' thing with my family, or maybe just like I *wish* there was – didn't know until the next day what started it: downed power lines sparking on a drought-dried field near a main arterial.

I was trained as a child to always tell a grownup when we saw "anything weird" with the power lines. I believed that they were where fire really came from, so, of course, I did my due diligence every time I saw power lines that were too low or touching a tree branch or had too many birds sitting on them. Twice I reported tennis shoes tied together hanging from them. I got so crazy searching for defective power lines that I began to imagine or hallucinate them falling when they weren't falling. Did I secretly *want* this to happen? Did I start to want to pull them down myself so I wouldn't feel like the only thing full of fire like my mom had communicated to me? Would finding such solidarity bring the change to who I was I

you want everything
your little sister
has to burn to
unrecognizable ash

needed and who my mom needed if I was going to get anything I wanted in life?

My mother, though nearly silent and meek, is a powerful woman in my pysche. I have known about her my whole life, yet to this day, who she is as a person remains entirely behind a firewall. She is the most hands-off mother I have ever encountered yet, she still controls my every move. She never said any of those words about who I am out loud – she never said many words at all no matter how many I offered her – but she never had to. Her silence was the gasoline to the fire that was me that she hated so much. I tell myself I will knock off the oversharing, the efforts to get her to fucking talk to me, if not love me and ratify my existence, which is her fault to begin with. Yet every time I'm given opportunity, out comes everything

I think about whatever subject she is querying me about. As with any emotion whatsoever, she literally does not respond, holding the line with a power I doubt I'll ever understand.

She asks me about the weather in my city when her phone app notifies her of a temperature she finds unusual or a forecast of heat and smoke (both unusual where I live now) but never how I am. *What are your plans this weekend?* she texts once or twice a month and I reflexively report on all the ways I'm moving forward since my divorce, all the status-quo pursuits to signify adulting, deftly managing her anxiety as I have since K was born just before I turned four. A therapist might suggest sororal resentment for the backbreaking burden of parental anxiety on a child. My mother will ask clarifying questions upon receipt of said report, but the minute I share anything personal, anything about feelings, or get fired up, she stops responding, drawing lines between her and intimacy miles out from her in every direction that has to do with me.

My internal monster wants to wrench those lines down on the parched acres of my soul to show her what never bringing the watering can of emotional care near one's children does to them. I remind my monster that these are the sorts of impulses that keep us having nothing. A therapist might suggest that being harsh with monsters may not be the most effective tactic to tame them.

What *do* you do with monsters, then? After my mother's performance check – when I was young and she was putting me to bed, she'd ask me if I brushed my teeth and then go feel my sink to check my answer before turning off the light after watching me tuck myself in – always as dry as a fire-starting field. Now, as soon as she gets her logistical fill from my recitals of my life, it's radio silence until her next sink check.

That sums up my three and a half decades of life. Or, said another way: though the piano was the only thing I thought about being okay – maybe even *wanted* to be okay – I hated piano lessons. They cut into my reading time, as did birthday parties, sleepovers and all the extra-curriculars my parents started "encouraging" me at age six to do to build my résumé. Plus, I wasn't that good at the piano, which meant I couldn't be the best. And being the best at everything one tried was the only way not to die alone under a bridge. I was good at reading, though. Maybe the best, depending on what the measuring stick was. I didn't read to escape but to learn the magic, the power behind the lines that drew me in and made me want to create the worlds and characters and words and stories that finally spotlighted all those who felt invisible even as they were on fire. I read so I could write. But writing wasn't a real job, so I snuck it in everywhere I could – in the back of math class, on the playground at recess. I couldn't sneak it in during piano, though. Lessons were nothing more than unredeemable hours of suck made of insecurity and hobbled children's songs and upon which nothing could be built.

For the half day we – there's that mirage of solidarity again – believed my sister's house and everything she owned was fire food, I steadied my shaking hands by "playing" Hot Cross Buns; the simple, boring parts of Chopsticks, and switching between the parts of the Heart and Soul duet on the kitchen counter. This kept me from cloaking in logistical questions to my mom about K + L + B + cat's whereabouts pleas for her acknowledgment that I am okay as exactly the person I am, that she wasn't mad that I threatened her life twice as I was making my way into the world, that she wasn't ashamed of my continued struggle to do so even after 35 years in it, especially compared to my sister who was only just now thinking she'd lost everything.

Then again, I'd never thought I had anything to lose except something I hated until I believed it was on fire. I don't need a therapist to point out that it's worked the opposite way when it comes to how I've felt about the live wire that is myself and that maybe it's time to get a watering can for that parched internal field myself.

KAYLA RANDOLPH

When in the Multiverse

Somewhere I am atop a block with a medal around my neck,
    in a skin-tight leotard
    receiving a knowing wink from the coach
    who's loved me since I was nine years old

Somewhere I am spinning on ice,
    loving the cold
    not just finding it home because of hockey helmets or New England
        roots
    but finding it mine

Somewhere I am swaddled in a black dress
    six feet underground
    bathed in tears
    and the shame of the Catholic Church

Somewhere I am in love with the boy from eighth grade,
        lucky enough
        to love him
        at the right time

Somewhere both my parents drove me to college,
        and my mother and I didn't have
        to struggle to lift the refrigerator on our own

Somewhere I am going to church every Sunday,
        in a floral dress
        saying my prayers
        thanking God for my life

But I am here.
And here,

I wonder about somewhere.

JENNIFER LEBLANC

Acedia, Sloth

In response to Hieronymus Bosch's The Seven Deadly Sins and the Four Last Things.

Sloth is the easiest.
It is so easy to do nothing,
to want nothing –
or at least to not want much at all.
Sloth is the easiest guest to please.
A seat by the small fire and to leave him alone.
Little more will be required.
Sloth is a cat yawning mid-stretch in the sun.
Sloth is a dull blade and depression.
When you approach him with demands,
when the room tilts and two unlit candles
perched like sad tulips in a varnished brass jug
gasp like hairline fractures,
there is no answer.

DAVID P. MILLER

When I am asked

what are my hopes
for Eternity? I must
demur. I can't say.
Eternity is merely massive.
Nothing there to grab
onto. Does it begin
with my redeemed corpse
startled from the ground?
I'm not that enamored
of this body bag.
Never have been. Cremation
seems a humbler choice.
Here's a better question:
who built this deep-drawered
sewing table, drop-leaf family
antique re-homed to our
kitchen? It's good work.
It has breath, muscle,
wrought into it. Four
legs that stand sure
in real time. If
I were asked about
real time, I might
reply, which of us
will revert to soil
first? Possibly the table.
But most likely me.

MAX HEINEGG

Dear Thalia Z.

Fingers in the lint of the Internet's purse,
I find you thirty years ago, edging axes with Chris,
whisper to grit on TT's house 58,
the sound of Come as reverie. *Now we sing*
so softly, deeply into the afterglow
of youth's loadout, oil-lipped from Hi-Fi, lit
on well whiskey & the dust of the stalls, bullshitters
on Brookline St. wheeling combos & half-stacks
into the Sound Museum at 2AM, ears feeding back,
pockets lined with ones, resolved to a feathered
minor chord. Ah, for the long-swept ashes
to burn again. Your songs remind me
of nights I thrilled but readied to end,
waiting for the pillow to cradle my head.

BLAKE KILGORE

Oncology Ward Irregulars

"Remove not the old landmark; and enter not into the fields of the fatherless."
— *Proverbs 23:10*

The brave souls in the children's hospital will not abandon
their post. Brain cancer patients hovering the grave
can't be cast into the fire storm of civilian-
targeting missiles and vacuum bombs.

Even the healthy children are dying young, smashed
under falling buildings. Some
incinerated little boys and girls, together with their grandmoms,
can't be found; maybe it's all just a nightmare.

Yes, and today's docket includes more war crimes, breaches
of international law, but the Pale Moth flutters on, undeterred
by the crumbling of the ruble or the seizure of his enemies' enemies' yachts. He's hiding
down at the far end of one of those absurdly lengthy tables.

His penny-pinchers keep resuscitating his fables to reassure him, and his
marionette journalists are smiling and talking fast, propping a Lost Cause
to his people. We had one of those here, and found it easy to look away, look away, look away.
When will the righteous Bear rise up to slay its master?

What happens when the backup generators die? Maybe the doctors
should send sickly daughters and sons to join the other
orphans. They could all meet up near the rubble
of an old schoolhouse for science class, form an assembly-line

for Molotov cocktails. This too we can all observe
on our televisions, tablets and phones, continents away, on couches
in living rooms or loveseats in dens. Some of us might want to slip in
to bed with our liquor to drown out the shame.

Talk about reality TV.

Nothing more can be offered, not at this time.
No air support, no troops, just kind
words and averted eyes, but it's hard to look away
from the flickering of light, the rising tide,
the darkening of night, last
heartbeats, and nowhere to hide.

PACELLA CHUKWUMA EKE

my step mother becomes the reincarnation of a cursed mortal

some times in march – that's today –
i stole my way into my neighbor's house
for wifi; see if it's possible for one to turn
others into stone
(and some random snake head dominated the screen)
perhaps this one's her mother
or her mother's mother
perhaps she still wears the genes
of this so-called *Medusa*
some times in march – that's today –
i do not know the difference between
my brother and a beast
because the night he had looked at father's wife
in that scale of rage she call eyes;
her rod had turned him into a beast-like vessel
nursing a stone for a heart

CYNTHIA BARGAR

Transmutation

Brew bronze & brass   & what is
alchemy?   Blizzard-bingeing
Law & Order SVU   as Al inks
      a stick & poke   above my left wrist.

They use acupuncture needles for that precise thin line.

            Circle   with a center dot.   Triangle
   crowned   &   filigree flourished.
Symbol for gold.   Gold being the goal:
   secret recipe   elixir
for eternal life   perfection of all matter.

Al's knuckles sport four of the five elements.

      I crave all seven metals.   The mystical mathematics
   64 hexagrams   magico-religious implications
weirdness   witchiness.   Plus inked at home holy.
   Like a home birth.   But no ritual.   Secularized by TV
detectives   rapists   sex workers   lawyers.

Nothing to do with beauty. Nothing to do with god.

JOANI REESE

Hromada*

(a whole in pieces
for the people of Ukraine)

I: Moscow

They polish words
that do not shine
coupled with cruelty
bound by trope
their twisted tale
of foes friends foes
blunts clumsy feints
toward honest prose
upchucked from tyrants'
liquid mouths who profit
most from snuffing lives
and sweep aside youth's
fruitful years to fumble
for a fist of earth, gone fallow
under February's stars.

II: Donbas

Draftees backpack lethal loads,
some fly spy drones, march southeast roads
to scarify a country, unremarkable
two months ago.

We eyeball screens, dreamy with gore.
Swift Migs hurl shells that rupture, tear.
As sirens blare, we savor snacks.
A billion techno fools watch war unwind.

Our darkened rooms display death, Live!
Most watch in benumbed ennui.
Ukraine unpacks worn guns and garb
while puppet Russian boys depart

their homes for tanks thrust
toward the sun-bright south –
Ripe sheaves of wheat will burn again
as soldiers set Donbas aflame
the same flame that they lit in 2014.

III: Mariupol

The press reports one woman's
curse that Ukraine's golden sunflowers
burst like arrows from the bloody breasts

of Russia's uninvited guests, aslant across
the cobblestones that once composed the lanes
of Mariupol, and now there's no one left
to rape or kill.

Fatigue from three pandemic years
enshrouds the world and wearies fear;
COVID expunged six million lives
this new war thrums the body count.
Retreat impacts a factory whose steel
can't block trajectories that murder
with impunity. The victor or the vanquished,
who will tell?

IV Kharkiv and Fastiv

Her camera captures shadow girls who leak from their respective shells.
Gashed by marauders, sullied skin can never be stitched right again.
Healing delayed's an empty cup and sluggish aid can't cover up
the dead spread under midwives' sheets, the disemboweled
who drape the streets of Kharkiv and Fastiv.

V: Dnipro

Ripples, once small, gather in power, soon shrapnel seeds
those yellow flowers in boys who scream before they break.
Face rictified with how he died, one young man can't reverse
his plunge from primacy to lumpen meat that smears the blasted brick
of Dnipro.

VI: Bucha

Civilian death discovered all around
this town Russia has fouled. New battle
lines appear as babies howl for mothers

gone who cannot comfort them again.

Pink girls ascend a bullet-riddled wall,
eye journalists who stiffen where they fell.
Church bells wail over Bucha, then stop still.

VII: Cherkasy

Sly, covetous oppressors lie,
deny atrocities nearby as endings
lurch toward dates we cannot name.
Remorse never revived rent flesh.
Limbs fetal-curl beneath the sky.
We gape and shake our heads a world away,
watch lives unfurl and furl in Cherkasy.
Who will revenge the wizened child
green eyes pried wide, future erased,
the question she'll forever ask,
"Was I just born too early, or too late?"

VIII: Kherson

Ships burn in port,
smoke blackens tongues.
Bone children tread
on shattered glass.
Kherson, now home
to no one but the dead.

VIIII: Kyiv

With ammunition flowing in, a fatigued man, face gaunt with strain, refuses to concede
another inch. The world first thought him callow, soft, expected him to scurry off to
someplace safe in exiled luxury. Two months go by, no longer naïf, the man still helms
this ship of state despite the odds predicting swift defeat. The world astonished that
Ukraine still meets each sun, courage the same, to best a man bereft of empathy. Some
heroes spring whole from necessity. One could not guess, much less predict, this man
would shoulder history, pick up a sword and reverse destiny.

*Hromada: *community* (Ukrainian)

KRIKOR DER

HOHANNESIAN

The Collywobbles.

Seven decades ago, world war
    in strange-sounding places –
        Tarawa, Monte Cassino, Stalingrad...

a trip to the docks in Boston Harbor
    to see the fleet being readied -
        destroyers, tankers, troop carriers

and the lone dinghy, unmoored,
    tossed on the harbor chop,
        helpless flotsam at tide's mercy

a look back at that dwarfed boat,
    when my skull met the oak piling,
        a muzzle-burst of stars before my eyes

a fusillade of cannon fire in the ears,
    the sights, the sounds an assault on
        the senses, I cast adrift in the wake,

sensibility scarred for life as by
    first exposure to combat - the mind may
        try to forget, but the cells hold the memory

and today the thunder of war still crackles,
    only the theaters have changed –
        Gaza, Kyiv, Aleppo...

The Raw Recruit

ROSE

CULLEN

Half his skull had been blown away. He was one of the new Auxiliaries, recruited from the demobbed soldiers, wearing a mix of police and army uniform, his distinctive tam o shanter was ripped to shreds and lying in the gutter, sodden with a mix of blood and the contents of his head.

Johnny flinched but tried to keep the bile from rising, it wouldn't do to puke up breakfast on his first day. He had seen dead bodies before of course, his father in his coffin only the year before, but not like this, not with the brains congealing on the pavement, one glazed eye staring up at the heavens. This must be the sort of thing his brother Willie had seen at Ypres, day after day, before he lost both his legs and his wits. Poor Willie, sitting by their mother's hearth muttering into his cup of tea and every so often there would be a little sob and wet cheeks. Johnny had been too young to enlist for The Great War but now, two years after victory, he was the one in uniform, the dark green of The Royal Irish Constabulary with a Webley revolver at his belt. And all across Ireland, his uncle said, they were facing another war and this was Johnny's chance to serve his King and Country. Looking down at this wreckage of a man on Belfast's Royal Avenue, Johnny wondered if the poor fellow had ever imagined such an ending, having survived the trenches of Flanders.

District Inspector Cousins arrived on the scene and drew up beside him, 'They'll pay for this, by God they will!'

An hour or so later five of them had been gathered by Cousins, Sergeant Dickson, another constable and two of the Auxiliaries. The Inspector patted Johnny on the back like he was showing him a great favour, 'I knew your father, Constable Smythe, a good man, staunch in his faith.'

They were going to pay a call on a known troublemaker over in West Belfast. According to the Inspector this man they were going to arrest, Jeremiah Barnes, had been imprisoned after the Rising. He went by the name Dermot now and called himself a politician; had the temerity to stand for Sein Fein at the General Election and got the drubbing he deserved but more recently he'd managed to get onto the Corporation.

'Protestant stock converted to papacy.' Inspector Cousins shook his head in disbelief. 'A traitor is what he is but we'll have him now.'

'Do you think he's the man responsible for the killing, sir? Johnny asked.

Cousins' look set hard, 'There isn't a one of these Sein Fein, that isn't responsible.'

An icy wind gusted up the Falls Road as they disembarked from the wagon. A murky day was giving way to the dark smudge of night; the gas lamps yet to be lit. Johnny shivered with the cold but also the thrill of his first taste of active service.

At a nod the men drew their revolvers from their belts. Johnny fumbled to release his own Webley and then gripped it tight. The Sergeant stepped forward to the entrance of a detached property and began to pound on the door.

In the silence between each barrage the sounds of scuffle were heard beyond. At last, it was opened by a woman clutching a baby at her shoulder.

'Where's your husband, Mrs Barnes!' Sergeant Dickson barked.

The baby screwed his face and wailed.

'Gentlemen ...' a voice from behind revealed a tall man pulling up his braces.

The guns were levelled against him.

The woman made the sign of the cross as he drew alongside.

'Are you going to shoot me in front of my wife?'

For a moment Johnny wondered if that was what was about to happen.

'You've questions to answer Mr Barnes.' Inspector Cousins pushed through across the threshold with the men streaming behind checking the parlour as the couple were ushered down the hall into their kitchen.

Cousins nodded to the Auxiliaries, 'Search the property.' And then to Johnny, 'Bring everyone down here.'

Johnny followed in the wake of the man who stomped up the stairs yelling for the occupants to come out with their hands up. A door edged ajar and a slight young girl, fourteen or so, appeared with her younger sister clutched to her skirts. He caught the look of terror on their faces and offered a smile of reassurance.

'It's all right, we won't hurt you, come on downstairs to your mammie.'

From another bedroom the Auxiliary prodded four small boys out onto the landing, 'God – don't they breed like rats!'

The oldest boy tugged away from the Auxiliary's rough grasp and aimed a kick at his shins receiving an angry wallop around the head in exchange.

Johnny reached out towards the boy before the Auxiliary could strike again, 'Come over here to me; what's your name?' he asked kindly.

'Padraig.' The boy rubbed at his sore ear; his eyes smarting.

'I'm Joe!' a lad about six years old piped up with a grin, taking Johnny's outstretched hand.

He herded the children down the stairs, the sounds of breaking glass and crashing furniture coming from the parlour. Behind him he could hear a similar rampage. The Auxiliaries had certainly set about searching every nook and cranny. Johnny shook his head at the wanton destruction but then it was one of their own that had been assassinated that day. He nudged the children into

---

Is it the *murder gang* you are – come to shoot me in the back

---

the kitchen. They immediately rushed across to their anxious mother who was hushing the baby. Joe clung to his hand. Johnny gave it a squeeze and whispered, 'Go over to your mammie now.'

Cousins was shouting down at the man perched on a stool, 'Last night – where were you?!'

Dermot Barnes shook his head with a wry smile.

'It's names we want Mister – start giving them up.' Cousins' livid features pressed closer.

Sergeant Dickson poked the prisoner's shoulder with his revolver to underline the demand.

'Is it the *murder gang* you are – come to shoot me in the back and say I resisted arrest? Like poor Michael. Isn't that the tactics of the Cromwell Club?'

The Inspector snorted. 'You'd be advised to co-operate.'

Johnny frowned, what was the man talking about? The Cromwell Club? What was that?

Dermot Barnes set his lips tight.

The Auxiliaries returned, both shaking their heads, nothing found.

Cousins looked with a conspiratorial eye from one officer to another, 'Maybe you need loosening up, is that it? I've heard you're a fíor Ghael and your brats are great for the dancing, will you not give us a show?'

The man stared boldly back.

A shot was fired into the floor. Johnny's eyes widened as another and another were discharged by the man's feet.

With a gasp of horror, the wife leapt to her feet; the children quaking beside her.

'Now you'll dance for me!' Cousins sneered.

Dermot Barnes rose to his feet towering over his interrogator.

'Please, sir, for the love of God!' It was his wife.

Johnny felt every muscle tense, what would happen now?

Slowly the man began to shuffle his feet, never taking his eyes from the Inspector.

'Sir, I must use the privy.' It was the wife again, urgent.

Cousins jerked his head, 'Take her out – be sure and watch her!'

She handed the baby over to the older girl and edged towards the back door, a fearful glance directed to her husband.

He nodded a reassurance and then cast a beaming smile back to his terrified children, 'Come on will we give these fellas a jig!' He clapped his hands, and stamped his feet. Joe was first to follow and then a toddler leapt up and down in imitation of a dance.

'Good lads!' Their father encouraged.

The door was opened which let out into the dark yard lit only by the spill of the gas burner from the window. The constable gestured for the woman to step outside.

'Foscail doras an chlóis! Éirinn go brath!' her husband called after her.

Immediately, Sergeant Dickson pistol-whipped him across the face, 'Shut your filthy Fenian mouth! You'll speak English or nothing at all!'

An Auxiliary lunged forward and landed a sucker punch in the gut, 'And you can take that for your fucking Republic!' The constable lingered at the back door a moment to enjoy the spectacle.

As Dermot Barnes doubled over, Cousins grabbed his chin, 'Are you ready to sing yet?'

'Or, will you dance to another tune?!' Sergeant Dickson jeered.

Johnny could hear the cries and yelps of the children at the sight of their father's bloodied nose. He knew there was a job to be done but he could

'Foscail doras an chlóis! Éirinn go brath!'

wish the Inspector might not conduct this brutal interrogation in front of the little ones.

As if in answer Cousins straightened his shoulders, 'Enough of the fun and games, men, let's get this bastard in handcuffs and out into the wagon.'

The woman was returning through the back door.

'Say goodbye to your husband, Mrs Barnes, you'll be lucky if you ever see him again!'

She approached her husband and laid a hand on his chest, 'God go with you!' she said slowly and with a quiet dignity.

Johnny felt a sudden surge of admiration. Where another might have been hysterical, this woman held herself together for the sake of her children, her husband. It seemed to break the man. Suddenly, his face collapsed and his shoulders slumped.

'Raise your hands for the cuffs!' the Sergeant ordered.

Dermot Barnes did as requested, then slid a humbled look towards Cousins. 'Before ... please, can I not use the privy also?'

'Ah – the big man is shitting himself now!' exclaimed one of the Auxiliaries and his fellow roared with a frantic laughter.

The Inspector gave a brusque nod towards Johnny, 'Take him outside – don't let him out of your sight!'

Johnny levelled his revolver and the prisoner stepped from the kitchen with head bowed. He hurried up the dimly lit yard to where the washhouse and privy were situated. Johnny followed briskly.

A door was already slightly ajar, 'I'll be but a moment, constable.' He stepped through and closed it behind him modestly.

It was a second or two before Johnny's eyes fully adjusted to the darkness of the yard, then he discerned there were two doors at the rear of the property. He lurched forward with a sickening premonition and flung open the one through which the prisoner had passed. It opened on to an alley.

The message in Gaelic shouted to his wife! To unlock this escape. They had been hoodwinked. Johnny threw himself into the passage, gun raised. He could see the silhouette of the man rushing towards the exit onto the now gas lit street. He could shoot him in the back; his aim was good enough. Isn't that what the Inspector wanted, a man resisting arrest?

'Halt!' Johnny screamed. 'Halt!!'

The man turned his head briefly at the end of the alley.

Now was the moment. Johnny's heart pounded. His arm dropped to his side. Dermot Barnes was gone.

Sergeant Dickson rushed out from the yard.

'Sorry, sir.'

'Fuck! Ye fucking idiot Smythe!'

'I thought it was the privy door ...'

'Damn and blast – we should have had the house surrounded!'

Cousins thumped his fist into his palm as he approached, 'Constable, that's a big fish you've let slip!'

Johnny hoped the Inspector could not see the bloom of red which suffused his cheeks.

They returned two hours later. In plain clothes. Cousins had his little terrier with him. He would have the dog with him all the time if he could, Dickson remarked to Johnny. That wasn't all. They were armed with cans of paraffin oil.

Dickson banged on the door and shouted through the letterbox, 'You've ten minutes to be out of the house!'

The commotion so late at night alerted the neighbours either side and before Mrs. Barnes had shepherded her flock through the front door the alarm was raised.

Johnny turned away from the look of puzzlement and distress in young Joe's eyes. His ears rang with the din and clatter of dustbin lids banging on the road, saucepans knocked against each other. He felt unnerved by the angry discordant sounds as he and the other men sprinkled paraffin around the front rooms of the house. The dog ran about in circles yapping at their feet.

'That'll do!' Cousins called out to them from the entrance and whistled for his dog; he clearly didn't want to linger with the dangers of an ambush.

As Johnny stepped back from the house, the Inspector handed him a box of matches.

Johnny didn't hesitate – he had made the wrong decision earlier in the day now he would make the right one.

He struck the light, watched the Sulphur flare and lit the soaked rag which was tossed into a pool of paraffin.

Flames whooshed up.

The blaze illuminated his slow smile of satisfaction.

AMY HOLMAN

Breathing Space

We turn out over the Atlantic, where one white sail sliver
and one bright skirt of speed give speckle to ultramarine

elsewhere emptied of boats, near 9:00, hanging north
to start the long descent to Boston, widening east

to adjust for the stretched diagonal downward to meet
coordinates of far runway – shifts that feel as if I'm folded

tightly to an origami square balloon, then inflated to each
angle, ear and eye, now falling, floating in place –

when I see the miniature shape of large black whale
inhaling air in JetBlue's rhyming shadow this August morn

traveling again, likely in a pod diving and rising east
of my spy, but out of sight on our next tilted turn.

MEG MCCARNEY

while my mother thinks we're having sex in the basement, we're really talking about dying

the bodies aren't cold yet, but they're making plans
to sail away after the service. the trash is collecting flies
because the diner won't let us share their dumpster.
we've given up on talking horses, frogs, and rainbow
dreams, although we have found pixie dust that makes us fly.

what's love going to do to stop the 77 bus
from crashing into the telephone pole, brandy's baby
from dying, my father from leaving?

there's no jam-and-biscuits breakfast that can save
us, no affectation big enough to make a difference
except cruelty. I promise to stop kissing
our landlord's feet and spit on them instead.

it costs $400 for a miracle at the clinic, but fifteen
hundred for rent. the office phone was out of battery —
you held the nurse's hand until it felt like mom's,

waddled home with bruises so deep you knew
at the end of your life, you'd still come up purple.

remember how chloe died tangled in the telephone
cord, calling the boy she loved to tell him it was too late?
we don't know anyone from the heartland
but already, we hate all of them.

invoking god's name in whole-note screams, we rattle
picture frames cursing the dead and ignorant. mom calls
from the upstairs doorway – we can't answer, too heavy.
we're carrying centuries of negligence in our lungs,
our battered grandmothers in our prefrontal cortexes.

we'll make up some excuse later; we're used
to sweet-talking to save a life. to be a woman
is to be the bouquet but moonlight as the vase,
always a refuge. you've got to be lenient to be fun,
so relax your borders, say *hello, come inside, don't bother
wiping your shoes, there are more people in line behind you.*

ANASTASIA VASSOS

Taking Off Billy Collins' Clothes

After 'Taking Off Emily Dickinson's Clothes' and with gestures toward borrowed lines

First, the glasses lifted off his bald head
as if his head had eyes, one gray hair
stuck in the nose piece
a few more on top.

And his shirt
cottoned or polyester, plastic
buttons undone, one by one
sweat stains 'round the pits.

Then, the pleated trousers
more complex than a seven-line stanza
with a belt unbuckling
such a stark affair
the zipper stuck like a log
in the river's bend
before my hand could grab hold.

You will want to know that
he was eating peach cobbler
on his La-Z-Boy in the den
droopy-eyed, those pleated trousers
'round about his ankles.

I proceeded like Eve
treading through the worn elastics
of his greyish tighty-whiteys,
finding the peduncle
– what a sturdy stalk –
ripping a hole
as I wedgied those Jockeys™
over his large head.

Naturally, I cannot tell you everything –
the way the glasses fell on the floor
and the trousers lay in a wrinkled heap,
but not before I thumbed through
the French-English dictionary
to look up the word *canard*.
You can believe I then proceeded cautiously.

What I can tell you is
we sailed around the room
across the bumpy ridges
of those hilltops such as they were
flattened by time's cruelty
in that Naugahyde jungle.

I could plainly see the poet drop
his cobbler, the aimless drip
of peaches

and I could hear him sigh
caesuras of common speech
his tears urging the process along.

Reader, we know that love is aimless
that a thesaurus is not a dinosaur
and that trust is a plank we hope will hold.
But breach of trust….
well.
That's the trouble with poetry
written by a genius
in the suburbs of Cleveland.

ELIZABETH VRENIOS

novena

a prisoner's constraint

name me raven
name me crow
raven name me
name me omen
name me amen
name me neon
omen name me
crow name me
name me one's own

razzamasazz moon
i wear an ocean's
mania in maroon
i own river's increases
moss's rise
moss's ceases
a wise survivor
i am a mirrored venus
a maximum varoom

i'm no rose
no never zero
no eerie sun
no worm cower
i'm no vermin sneeze
no one's sour
never seen camaro
nor snow-worn sorrow

i soar over sunrise seasons
in cosmic crimson
scream arias
in universe's sea
i am a cross
in sin's novena
i am a neon amen
i am woman
i am no crime

Excerpt from

The eviction notice set all their sorrows into motion. Joseph understood that now in ways impossible to appreciate let alone understand as a shy, nervous kid of ten and a half that April in 1958. Too mesmerized then by his older brother Michael, the four years stretched between them like a lifetime, to resist the larger forces remaking their lives.

He discovered the notice folded in a pocket of Michael's denim jacket late one afternoon, hoping to find enough loose change for a pack of Hot Tamales from the candy store on Hale Street. The Boston Redevelopment Authority had mailed the same letter to every resident of the West End earlier that week, announcing the coming destruction of the world they knew. Joseph's parents had read aloud portions of the BRA's threat in exasperated bursts of Italian and English across the kitchen table. The government had at last taken the neighborhood – all forty-eight acres of it. Seized under eminent domain.

Displaced

OLIVIA KATE CERRONE

Neighbors argued from stairwells and in doorways, skeptical that the redevelopment would even happen this time. Years of uncertainty had hardened their cynicism – the city's plans moving back and forth in a confusing bureaucratic shuffle, heralding a tiresome series of preliminary and final approvals in a long, inane process that seemed to bear no real consequences on their own lives. So many previous announcements had provoked a similar upset, inspiring a flurry of community meetings and protests, though no demolition crew appeared in the streets. Delays and empty threats. Why should this time be any different? Life would continue as it had before, the neighborhood enduring, untouched.

Still, there'd been talks of protests. Marches to City Hall. Threats of violence. An address marked in red absorbed Joseph, one scribbled in Michael's sloppy handwriting beneath the letter's typeface. 42 Staniford Street. No place he recognized. What did his brother have in store?

The apartment buzzer squealed. Joseph stuffed the eviction notice into his back pocket in a quick, unthinking way, and returned his brother's jacket to the closet they shared. He sat on his bed, his pulse throbbing and pretended to read a Superman comic. Michael wouldn't be home for at least another hour, but he was known to defy any schedule imposed upon him. The masonry apprenticeship their father had arranged was supposed to straighten him out. How volatile he'd become since leaving school that winter, arriving home more than once with a black eye and bloodied knuckles.

His mother's high heels tapped across the kitchen floor. Coffee percolated. Warm roasted scents pervaded through the rooms. She greeted Myra Horowitz, who lived on Poplar Street, her voice bright with welcome. Another visitor from the Committee. She seldom spoke of her involvement with the organization and their efforts to save the West End. His mother often read aloud Mrs. Horowitz's letters published in the local papers, always so impressed by her friend's arguments against the redevelopment, and how West Enders took pride in their neighborhood, fighting to use money left in a trust to build an extensive recreation area near the Charles River, contributing to those seasonal joys that Bostonians cherished – sailing excursions and concerts at the Hatch Shell among them. How his mother repeated her words with passion. She'd carved out another identity altogether through the Committee, resisting the small, aproned existence which consumed most other mothers he knew – slipping off to meetings and protests in and around her domestic chores.

Joseph tossed his comic aside and dug out the wooden cigar box hidden in a drawer full of Michael's socks. He emptied the small collection of pocketknives atop his bed and sorted through them, unable to find the Ka-Bar with its rounded brown handle fit together with leather washers and a curving, pointed blade strong enough to dig trenches, force apart nails and crates or disembowel someone in one decisive swipe.

Michael had winked over the last detail, claiming also that he'd somehow purchased the combat knife from some local pawnshop with so many of them floating around after the war. Who knew how he'd really obtained it, which captivated Joseph's imagination like nothing else, knowing it had once belonged to a real soldier. Now its absence made him nervous, hungry for his brother's plans.

He examined the other knives, their blades no longer than the spread of his palm. He flicked them open and shut the way his brother had shown him with a quick flip of the wrist. Sunlight caught in their handles' iridescent pearl inlay. He fingered one of the duller edges just to see how hard he could press skin against blade before splitting flesh.

"Let them try it." His mother forced his attention. "Eight weeks is not enough time to evict twenty thousand people. What do they think they'll do? Drag us out?"

Joseph left the bedroom, unsettled, and stood in the hallway, hidden against the wall as he strained to listened, dancing a pocketknife between his hands. Apartment noises permeated their walls with television dramas, shouting voices, and baby wails. Cooking smells forever wafted through the floorboards, along with the harsh ammonia and bleach concoction that kerchief-headed Mrs. Polansky used, scrubbing the building's stairways. One could not excise themselves from the intimacy of their neighbors.

"Just weeks ago, the city was repaving our streets and installing new gas meters in all the apartments. Now what sense does that make?" Mrs. Horowitz said.

"They won't go through with it. I don't believe it. You remember this?" His mother rustled some papers. He imagined the old blue shoebox she kept on her nightstand, one full of newspaper clippings and pamphlets tracing the progression of the West End's redevelopment plans. She kept a similar box full of documents related to his late grandfather's long-ago trial, hidden under her dresser. He'd rifled through it once while she was out grocery shopping. The scandal he wasn't allowed to discuss.

"Here it is," she said. "1956. Demolition in eight months. Relocation of all West End residents before the end of the year. Never happened."

Mrs. Horowitz sighed, soft exasperation straining her words. "Even so, we need to organize people. There's still time."

Coffee spoons clinked against saucers. More paperwork shuffled. A kitchen chair scraped across the floor. Joseph's mother hummed a note of concern.

"Oh, Myra, I don't know. Half of them can't read enough English to understand it. They'd get suspicious."

"That's exactly what the BRA has counted on, preying on people's ignorance. Confusing them with bad information in the press. If more were involved in our efforts, we'd help them better. They need us." Mrs. Horowitz tapped out the last three words, and Joseph pictured her knuckles rapping against the side of the table. She spoke of a mother's march at City Hall, one that his own could help lead.

Life happened in the street.

"You have a deep connection to this community, Giulia. More so than our Committee leaders even. It's why the West Enders never took a real shine to us. Not like they should've. But there's still time. If other families see you out there, they'll want to participate too."

Joseph's mother sighed, doubtful. "I agree we need to get more of them at the protests. But it makes some folks nervous getting too involved. Besides, the Committee's lawsuit against the city will stall the evictions."

"And what if it doesn't?" Mrs. Horowitz's voice gained an edge. "We need to send a message to Mayor Hynes and his gang of crooks. Make it clear that we all intend to stay in our homes for as long as possible."

Joseph pressed his thumb against the pocketknife's blade without thinking and nicked himself. He let out a small cry, dropping the knife against the hardwood floor. The women went silent for a moment before his mother called his name.

"I thought you were out with your friends? Come here."

A tiny bead of red sprouted from his skin. Joseph sucked the wound and returned the pocketknife to its cigar box, hesitant to leave the room. He knew well his mother's capacity for sudden rages. Once she'd chased him through the rooms with a wooden spatula, hollering curses, after he'd left his matchbox cars strewn across the living room floor. Hours later she apologized, lavishing kisses against his head and serving his favorite butter-sweet *pizzelle* cookies, their snowflake-inspired designs coated thick with powdered sugar.

He entered the kitchen, unable to meet his mother's probing gaze. Sunlight beamed through the windows over the sink, streaking through the faded lace curtains and across the pale-yellow cabinets. 'Save the West End Committee' flyers and other pamphlets were stacked on the small round table. Mrs. Horowitz adjusted her browline glass-

"Save the West End"

es and directed a small, prim smile at him as she ran a manicured hand along the auburn curls that tapered into a bob around her ears.

"Joey, what happened?" His mother rose from the table, smoothing down the folds of her green circle skirt as she approached him. Her thick dark hair, swept up and back in an elegant bouffant, appeared like a crown. He shrugged, embarrassed. She examined his cut, shaking her head. "Now how'd you do a thing like that?"

She ran the sink faucet over the affected finger and pressed a small dishrag against the wound, ordering him to hold it tight until the bleeding stopped. He did so, uncertain how to articulate his concerns about Michael or where they'd live if the city destroyed their home. She soon herded him toward the door and fit a quarter into his hand with instructions to be a good boy and fetch a nice watermelon ice for himself.

Life happened in the street. Boys played stickball in alleyways, the girls jumping rope or playing hopscotch, while women in faded plaid house dresses sat together on the stoops of crowded brownstones, whispering together, the occasional cigarette passed between them. Transistor radios played at their feet. Joseph searched beyond their heads, hoping for some glimpse of Michael. The Felman sisters from next door rushed past him on metal skates. The scrape of their wheels against asphalt pricked Joseph with want. Most West End kids possessed at least a scooter, some made of fruit boxes and soda bottle caps. He and Michael had once shared an old, busted-up two-speeder before the bike chain rusted off. Now they were both stuck on foot.

He followed the familiar curve of tall, brick rowhouses lining Pitts Street. West Enders shouted conversations at one another across the street, leaning from black-ribbed fire escapes or windows topped in arch-shaped lintels, while housewives clipped bed sheets, starched white shirts and limp undergarments to clotheslines strung high between apartments. Most of his own relatives lived within shouting distance. Joseph felt enmeshed within the community, tethered to everyone around. Various languages webbed between those he passed – the Jewish and Polish refugees displaced by the war; the Ukrainian, Greek, and Albanian families who operated small dry goods stores and luncheonettes. A mixed neighborhood, his mother called it. Somehow, folks got along. They even looked after one another sometimes.

Joseph crossed the street, past the kosher meat market with its gold Hebrew letters painted across the display windows, where a row of skinned chickens hung. Hot bread scents lingered in the air. Some of the storefronts appeared dark and empty, the lots vacant for months now. A young couple stood at the curb, watching a sofa hauled away by two heavy-set men into the back of a flatbed truck. Several old men gathered nearby at the corner of Merrimac Street, their hands and fingers stabbing the air, gesticulating toward the movers.

The city had turned against them.

CONNOR CASH COLBERT

One Hundred Smoots

Tell me about the day all the fish died in the Charles River.

Tell me about the sock in the drainpipe. How it flooded the basement.

Tell me a love story. You won't be gay forever. Think you'll be good in a few years.

It's just boredom. A city of glass bottles. Trapped and suffocated in an algal bloom.

Choked on superheated green. It only takes two degrees. Facts horrify me but

We have miles to go. Debts to pay. Moon like cheese. It's a lovely spaceship.

A terrarium dream. Mouthful of ketchup at liftoff. Come out to the edge

Of your humor's brackwater and wade far as you can stand. I believe love is patient.

I believe a dead fish is an omen. I believe a hundred dead fish is ecological collapse.

Tell me it's inheritance. Rage is indiscriminate. Tell me you tried to stop

The boys throwing basketballs on each flopping soul, which is not cheap,

Soul which is viscid and unchewable as the spit in your smile. Tell me

You're not a machine, not like me. Tell me this is a love story.

I believe in possibility. Mercy is a possibility. Lose track of days

In burning laundromats where God walks, tall as an ogre. He watches

The stars dim like rotting pears. Tell me his creatures die every day. I can forgive you,

Who will be good in a few years, if I just. Mouthful of socks tumble like dead fish.

River dried up. Whole neighborhood caught fire. They called a congressional hearing but

No one called the fire department. I believe in the possibility God sees every thing.

I believe it was boredom. I believe you were stronger. It's an inheritance story

But it's all relative fiction. Mercy is choosing. I can stop whenever I want, not like you.

I built this spaceship to tell you this: The difference between animal and machine is

The animal knows the difference.

DIANE POHL

The 67 Percent

There is a small town in the Commonwealth

Where real estate prices have out-paced all other towns

Where on Main Street
Lilly Pulitzer-clad tourists – mostly grown women with blonde hair – pose
in front of the Lilly Pulitzer store there wearing signature
Lilly Pulitzer colors which happen to share a palette with Barbie and unicorns
(hot pink, turquoise, purple, lime green) but where there are no rainbow flags in the July
4th 'Independence Day' parade

Where the property tax rate is the lowest of all towns

Where the town is surrounded by pristine ocean and sound waters
but there are more private swimming pools per capita than any other town

Where the number of people living in town is six thousand

Where the number of people living in poverty is four hundred and thirty

and

Where the percentage of children in the public school living in poverty is sixty-seven
percent.

ANNE MYLES

The Owl

Boston, Winter 1637-1638

One night in that long winter, all of you banished
but not yet gone, you looked up to the roofline
and saw the snowy owl: impassive white face,
wide eyes almost human. God's messenger,
you thought – such purity, such fierce intent.
It jolted you from worrying to stillness:
Lo, I am with you always. The last of one life now –
yet after all what did it matter to start over,
when anyone might judge you'd barely started?
Let your new world be new. You shifted your feet,
settled your shoulders, clicked softly in the dark.

But later, in bed, you hear the high screaming,
the deep hooting, the rustle of inexorable wings.
It goes on and on, but you do not wish it over.
You feel your talons, the sharp hook of your beak
darting and ripping. The ones you've lived among
who call you full of error. Who scorn the truth.
Let it be you. Let it be God. Let their false faith
lie limp and torn. Let them suffer first. Oh never
will you dare mention it by day – that ravening
to rise on your light bones then rocket down
with flawless sight, swift to their destruction.

ANNE MYLES

Dyer's Island

Narragansett Bay, 1639 / 2018

On the public launch near Portsmouth
wavelets break beneath the pier
the island named for William Dyer
lies in the distance   so low
it almost merges
with a larger island beyond

Light waves once rippled
off the hulls pushing southward:
we still know what that sounds like
and the male laughter   voices
in their accents odd to us
not hard to imagine

nor the boot-heel sinking into muck
the forearm holding back scrub

William saw it and wanted it:
twenty-eight and lusty
with hook and gun
one young son shooting a stick already
on his way to stake new land

How strange to know about desire
to behold the print of it
four centuries later:
thin dark rim
between bay and sky
where he longed to scribe his name

But what of Mary's Island
which has no date   lies on no map
just a wisp against the blue
as if you glimpsed the water parting
like a pair of lips to express it
then gone before you look again

terra incognita
I keep coming to back to
imagining if I watched patiently enough
I could see the truth of what she wanted
that was   and was not God

*"The Owl" and "Dyer's Island" come from a series of poems on the life of
Quaker martyr Mary Dyer (1611?-1660).*

LAURA GOLDIN

The Living

Against all odds and out of season
       winter.

       I was tending to my branches
I was in the forest
         counting rings.

Forgive me. What I wanted was
       nothing you brought me.   Also
I was wounded and
had grown so entirely cold.

It was not just the dead.
The living, too, gnawed at me
       like a saw-toothed, half-remembered thing.
And I had lost the impulse of repair.

Forgive me. I had moved
       so far past sleep, past all
our forms
of reckoning.

Such emptiness, the other
side of which
       was nothing

and was calling me.

Lessons

What is Buddha? a young monk asked.
Three pounds of flax, the Master said.

and if I begged he might add cacophonies
of cranky crows racing south and squirrels
splooting in reluctant trees and mountains
rising decorously through mizzling dawns
and the exquisite Black man strolling down
grocery aisles unaware of my awe
reflecting off freezer doors and my teenage date
kissing me until my father raged
the porch lights on and the shade tree mechanic
down the street fiddling with his brakes
to throbs of Sgt. Pepper and his lonely hearts
and everyone/thing I'll never see before
this life spins out and everyone/thing
waiting ecstatically for my rebound

ABDULRAZAQ SALIHU

On wishing reality was a healer

Cheers to blue serenity on the night of Qadr,
To the crescent moon like a broken plate,
To Ramadans bloom, dates and its sour age,
Chai and mud, to December's fair breeze
Breaking through the watered skin, to the old chair,
Brown faded furniture, the sand grains like body,
To purple hibiscus, the folding mountain,
The bloated, the youngest full moon ,
To buried virtues, the forsaken magnolia,
The outcast by the mouth of the shore,
Cheers to these, sorry we believed all would heal,
A big cheer to the new born escaping from
The heavens like honey.

EILEEN CLEARY

The Queen of Queens
by Jennifer Martelli

REVIEWS

Jennifer Martelli's *The Queen of Queens* was composed amid the turmoil of the Trump years, and hit the publication bin while the world was still reeling from the throes of COVID-19. And, it was born of the incessant war on women, which this poet, and anyone with eyes has witnessed since childhood. Therefore, these poems are appropriately as angry and as gritty as the battle in which women still fight to be heard. This book conjures the "women nobody heard."

Geraldine Ferarro has been quoted as saying, "Some leaders are born women." This book considers such leaders in addition to Ferarro: Nancy Pelosi, the speaker's mother and aunts, and Madonna. Also, the original Madonna, "the one with the pearl rosary moons on a tarnished chain."

Martelli personifies COVID-19 as a woman who has been ignored too long. "She holds sway, she lumbers/ like the Elephant Queen, the big tusker." And this royal bitch is taking no prisoners. "No one dares/ bump into this woman. She put on her red/pearl crown and everybody—are you/ happy now—has to watch her, listen/ to what she has to say." Throughout the book, the language is clear and direct.

These poems meet the world as it is and do not shrink from subjects such as drug use, abortion, anger, and politics.They dare to mingle the symbols of femininity with these issues which men have historically commandeered as matters they alone should govern. In "Watching Clips of the Democratic National Convention, July 19, 1984," we see Geraldine Ferraro accept the nomination to the Vice Presidency nearly forty years before Kamala Harris was sworn into office. Ferraro, decked in strands of decorative pearls, births new ambition and longing for the women in the audience who "reach their /arms up to her/wave and reach as if offered open-handed a merciful pearl."

Adding to Martelli's power is her mentioning of her menarche. No part of a woman's life is verboten in this book. "Last night my ghost period came to visit." This is vital because the speaker is trying not to disappear, and must not allow parts of the self to vanish as if they never existed. "Long ago I found the cure for disappearing." Read this collection from a master poet that gives voice to women, angry and feminine and real, these poems that are not "afraid of their tongues."

The Queen of Queens · **Jennifer Martelli**
VIA Folios, Bordighera Press, 2022;
ISBN 978-1-59954-180-8

GLORIA MONAGHAN

Far Cry, poems
by Tom Daley

REVIEWS

The word I use to describe Tom Daley's new collection, *Far Cry,* is joyful, which may sound odd given that the book is an elegy to an estranged old friend who has suddenly died. In these poems we find the all too familiar reluctance to let go of the past and the absolute necessity of looking back. I am reminded of Dante's line: "There is no greater sorrow then to recall our times of joy in wretchedness."Can we not all relate to one such love?

This book is a meditation on the whole kit and caboodle; the difficult, complicated, funny, and joyous. It is a nostalgic look into a life at a between adulthood and youth. Moreover, the book is an elegy and tribute to an old companion during a time when homosexual love was considered sinful. It is within this secret context, which society perverted, we find adoration, sex, longing, shame, anger and finally love.

Far Cry serves as an art form in itself; a delicious
little hand-crafted chapbook, reminiscent of
Frank O'Hara's *Lunch Poems*. The book is pub-
lished by *Ethel*, a mico-press, whose publisher is
Sara Lefsyk. Daley is also an exquisite calligra-
phist and visual artist and made his own cover
art. The imagery in these poems create a space
which already exists somehow in the mind of the
reader. Take for example "Second Tuesday,"

The moon lays its sheen
on the neighbor's slate roof

on the second Tuesday
after your death.

There is a religiosity about the subject matter.
The entire collection is written in couplets to hon-
or the lovemaking of lovers everywhere who see
and understand one another. Despite the faults
and *mealybugs*, love provides the final refuge.
Bend your mind to "Gay Blade":

How delicate the skin was
on your shoulder blades

any fierce hug would set it
astir with hurt fire ants

crambling themselves
into pockets and pores.

Here, old contender,
bring me your scalding

sashay. Bring me your
scolding sense of the proper

alignment of recent trends
in thermals and socks,

your eye always split between
nasturtiums and hawks.

Note the slant and not so slant rhymes. The thin-
ness of fire ants, the throatiness of sashay, and
the gutsy companion alive in this prayer all bring
us back to the summer of youth and nasturtiums
– "all your gone whispers/are grinning me down."
The epitaph, a grin to death, a smile knowing you
have lived it. And that is why this book is joyful,
and the memory delicious, in spite of everything,
"your hair was the color/of river sand."

The whole thing sings. Every Nerudaun turn
(thermals and socks) bring this friend back from
the shadow of death. Phil Herbert, the subject of
the book, died suddenly in 2020 according to the

preface. Daley puts the immediacy of Herbert's death into words in the poem, "A Grey Mouse has Drowned,"

A grey mouse has drowned
In the watering can.

It wanted, like you, to try
that last living thing

that would stave off a bursting thirst.
I have composted it.

Tom Daley has composted these memories into poems that are a revelation of beauty, and a recollection of sexual pleasure in youth. Later in the same poem, sitting on the toilet, the speaker recalls the backstairs to the shower they shared and the 'grey-green towel/on its hipbones'. There is so much poignancy mixed with joy:

...Your mouse-self noses
Its aquilined way into my jocund

expectation and I shimmer
the shower ions into a mirage

of you wreathing me with steam
of an unalloyed joy.

This book memorializes the complex difficult and beautiful Herbert, who can find the Infant of Prague in a brown paper bag, who chortles and crabs the speaker's ear. The subject's consideration and condemnation for others "You had a bedroom/set aside for snores." In the poem, "Accomplice to the Hours" there is the Orphic plea, the longing for the past, youth, passion, and love:

"Oh beloved boy skitter back

to me through your blood clots,
I am desperate

In the poem "I Address the Virtual Impossibility of Conjuring You with Verses that Are Merely Descriptive," we see the humor like ease in which the sacred and profane are wed together inseparably. Tom Daley's subject is hawklike, mustached, serious, but not so serious sex oozes from these pages:

...South of your belt,
your snake with its blue-jean hide

was a firebreak in the roughneck forest
of your crotch. To the north,

a khaki top or an immaculately
white t-shirt that you had probably ironed.

There were always men in the woodwork,
splintering or shying under the wide

rabbit trap of your eyes. Always
a feast being prepared

in the scorching pockets
of your salivary glands.

Always a haunch
waiting to be palmed,

a genuflection waiting
to be blessed.

The poem brings to mind the gay iconic figures of Saint Sebastian, Whitman and Frank O'Hara (on a lunch date or a picnic). The line breaks are perfectly timed yet unexpected. There is precision and economy of word choice, but what stands out to me are the use of verbs; palmed, aquilined. The way men under the woodwork are splintering and shying- all associated with the behavior of animals. How loving and accepting is this little treasure is taking us back into a time when a man loving a man was still a crime. This small gift,

sacred and well bound, is a true tribute to a love gone but never forgotten. There is nothing sentimental in this look back. There is the seductiveness of youth, the hot breath of goodbye. In "Am I Any Closer?" the poet asks the living ghost,

Call my name

with your confounded
affection, glower at me

with your roguish
admonishments, catch

your palms on the stubble
of my throat. I cannot

leave you to history.

Far Cry, poems · **Tom Daley**
Ethel Zine & Micro Press, 2022

Author Biographies

Cynthia Bargar is Associate Poetry editor at Pangyrus. Her poems have appeared or are upcoming in many journals including *Driftwood Press, SWWIM Every Day, Rogue Agent, Book of Matches*, and in the book, *Our Provincetown: Intimate Portraits* by Barbara E. Cohen (Provincetown Arts Press, 2021). Her poetry collection, *Sleeping in the Dead Girl's Room*, came out from Lily Poetry Review Books in January, 2022.

◎

Olivia Kate Cerrone has received numerous honors, including the Crab Orchard Review's Jack Dyer Fiction Prize and an American Fiction Award for her historical novella *The Hunger Saint*. Excerpts from her novel-in-progress, *Displaced*, were longlisted for both the 2022 DISQUIET Literary Prize and the Masters Review Novel Excerpt Contest.

◎

Chukwuma Eke Pacella, NGP Xv, is a Nigerian poet and the winner of the cradle poetry contest, F.O.W, the 1st runner up for the Nigerian Prize for Teen Authors Award and BKPW. She has contributed to several literary

magazines and poetry anthologies. She is also a member of the HillTop
Creative Arts Foundation.

◎

Connor Cash Colbert (he/him) is a human poet currently living on the tra-
ditional land of the Duwamish people past & present in Seattle. His poetry
can be found in *Dear Magazine, Vagabond City*, and *Not A Press*. Can be occa-
sionally found on twitter @con_siderthis and instagram @maggot_nelson.

◎

Eileen Cleary is the editor of *Lily Poetry Review* and author of *Child Ward
of the Commonwealth* (Main Street Rag Press, 2019), and *2AM with Keats*
(Nixes Mate, 2021).

◎

Rose M Cullen was born in Dublin and now lives in Manchester, England.
She has facilitated creative writing on residencies in psychiatric hospitals
and prisons. Numerous short stories and flash fiction have been published
online and appeared in anthologies. Her debut novel *The Lucky Country*, a
story of emigration set in 1960s Australia was published in April 2021.

◎

Krikor Der Hohannesian has published in over 275 literary journals
including *The South Carolina Review, Atlanta Review, Louisiana Literature,
Connecticut Review, Comstock Review,* and *Natural Bridge.* He is the author
of three books, *Ghosts and Whispers* (Finishing Line Press, 2010), *Refuge in
the Shadows* (Červená Barva Press, 2013) and *First Generation* (Dos Madres
Press, 2020).

Hadley Dion is a writer, audio editor, and filmmaker from Los Angeles. Her poems have been published or are forthcoming in *Scapegoat Review, Anti-Heroin Chic, FreezeRay Poetry, Jupiter Review, Remington Review, Bandit Fiction*, and more. She loves volunteering at her local cat rescue, ghost stories, and crafting punch needle rugs.

◎

Sara Epstein is a clinical psychologist from Winchester, Massachusetts. Her poetry collection, *Bar of Rest*, is forthcoming with Kelsay Books (2023). She has published in many journals including, *Mocking Heart Review, Silkworm, Paradise in Limbo, Mom Egg Review, Chest Journal, Literary Mama*, and two anthologies: *Sacred Waters*, and *Coming of Age*.

◎

Laura Goldin is a publishing lawyer in New York. Her recent poems appear or are forthcoming in *One Art, Right Hand Pointing, Molecule: A Tiny Lit Mag, Club Plum, Tiny Wren, Blue Heron Review, Driftwood, Rogue Agent, Shot Glass Journal, Minyan Magazine*, and *Maximus Magazine*.

◎

Max Heinegg lives, teaches, brews beer, and makes records in Medford, Massachusetts. His first book, *Good Harbor*, won the inaugural Paul Nemser Prize from Lily Poetry Press. His work has appeared in *32 Poems, The Cortland Review, Thrush, Nimrod, Twyckenham Notes*, and *Nixes Mate Review.*

◎

Amy Holman is a poet and literary consultant. She has five poetry books, including *Wrens Fly Through This Opened Window*, and the prizewinning chapbook, *Wait for Me, I'm Gone*. Recent poems have been in *The Ekphrastic Review*, and *The Chiron Review*, and flash fiction in *Club Plum*.

◉

Martha Jackson Kaplan is the recipient of the Zylpha Mapp Robinson International Poetry Award, an editor-in-chief award from *Möbius, The Poetry Magazine*, awards from the Wisconsin Fellowship of Poets, and has been nominated for a Pushcart. Recently published in *The Night Heron Barks*, more can be found at marthakaplanpoet.com.

◉

Blake Kilgore is the author of *Leviathan* (hapless hip books, 2021), a collection of poems. His writing has appeared in many fine journals, most recently in *Flint Hills Review, Frost Meadow Review*, and *Amethyst Review*. You can find out more at blakekilgore.com.

◉

Linda Lamenza is a poet and literacy specialist in Massachusetts. Her work is forthcoming or has appeared in *Mom Egg Review, Constellations, Rogue Agent, Main Street Rag, The Comstock Review, The Tishman Review*, and elsewhere. Her chapbook, *Left-Handed Poetry*, was a finalist for Hunger Mountain's May Day Mountain Chapbook Series.

◉

Jennifer LeBlanc earned an MFA in Creative Writing from Lesley University. Her first full-length book, *Descent*, was published by Finishing Line Press and named a Distinguished Favorite in Poetry (Independent Press Award). Individual poems have been published or are forthcoming in journals such as *Consequence* and *The Adirondack Review*.

Carolyn Martin is a lover of gardening and snorkeling, feral cats and backyard birds, writing and photography. Her poems have been published in more than 150 journals throughout North America, Australia, and the UK. She is poetry editor of *Kosmos Quarterly: journal for global transformation*. More information at www. carolynmartinpoet.com.

◉

Meg McCarney is a Boston resident, writer, and recent graduate of Lesley University. Her work is deeply concerned with the topics of trauma and complicity, sparking further social dialogues around sexual violence and abuse culture. She loves hedgehogs, oatmeal raisin cookies, and walking across town for good iced matcha.

◉

David P. Miller has published two books, *Bend in the Stair* (Lily Poetry Review Books, 2021) and *Sprawled Asleep* (Nixes Mate Books, 2019). His poems have recently appeared in *Meat for Tea, The Poetry Porch, subTerrain, Muddy River Poetry Review, Lily Poetry Review*, and *Constellations*, among others.

◉

Don Mitchell is a Black American poet and performer currently writing in Ellenwood, Georgia.

◉

Anne Myles has work in *On the Seawall, North American Review, Whale Road Review, Lavender Review,* and elsewhere. Professor Emeritus of English at the University of Northern Iowa, she holds an MFA from the Vermont College of Fine Arts. Final Thursday Press published her latest book, *What Woman That Was: Poems for Mary Dyer*.

Diane Pohl lives in Cambridge, Massachusetts, where there are books along the sidewalks. Her poems are published or forthcoming in The *Paterson Literary Review, The Lake, Slipstream, The Main Street Rag*, elsewhere. Her prose poem 'When you were 9' won an Allen Ginsburg Award.

◦

Kayla Randolph is a lover of words. Her piece "Tripping Since the '50s" won the award of "Distinction" in nonfiction at the 2021 Emerson College Senior Writing Awards. Her publication credits include *Brushfire Literature & Arts Journal, Calling the Beginning from Wingless Dreamer*, and Alyssa Milano's *Sorry Not Sorry* podcast.

◦

Joani Reese is a writer living in darkest Texas. Her cats keep her sane, most of the time.

◦

Gloria Monaghan is a Professor at Wentworth University. She has published five books of poetry. Her poems have appeared in *Nixes Mate, NPR, Poem-a-Day, Lily Poetry Review, Mom Egg Review*, among others. She has been nominated for the Pushcart Prize, the Massachusetts Book Award, and the Griffin Prize.

◦

Abdulrazaq Salihu he/him is a 17 year old Nigerian award winning writer,poet, essayist,spoken word artist and novelist.He's a member of the hill top creative arts foundation and was the recipient of the 2022 Masks Literary Magazine Poetry award .

Anastasia Vassos is the author of *Nike Adjusting Her Sandal* (Nixes Mate, 2021). Her chapbook *Nostos* will be published by Kelsay Books in 2023. *Nostos* (under a different title) was named a finalist in Two Sylvias' and Headlight Review's Chapbook Contests. Her poems appear in *Thrush, SWWIM, RHINO, Whale Road Review,* and elsewhere. She speaks three languages and lives in Boston.

◉

Ms. Kirkpatrick-Vrenios has twice been nominated for Pushcart awards. She published in various journals and anthologies. Her award-winning chapbook, *Special Delivery*, was published in the spring of 2016. Her second volume of poetry *Empty the Ocean with a Thimble* was released in April by Word Tech Communications.

◉

Megan Wildhood is a neurodiverse writer, editor and writing coach who thrives helping entrepreneurs and small business owners create authentic copy to reach the people they feel called to serve. She helps her readers feel seen in her poetry chapbook *Long Division* (Finishing Line Press, 2017) as well as *Yes! Magazine, Mad in America, The Sun* and elsewhere. You can learn more about her writing and working with her at meganwildhood.com.

Colophon

The text is set in Maiola, a contemporary typeface inspired by early Czech type design. The titles are set in Tablet Gothic, a grotesque sans-serif grounded in 19th century British typography. Both fonts were designed by Veronika Burian, a type designer and co-founder of the independent type foundry TypeTogether. She is also involved with Alphabettes.org, a showcase for work and research on lettering, typography, and type design by women.

SUBSCRIBE TO NIXES MATE REVIEW.

Get 2 issues per year for $25.
Go to nixesmate.pub/subscribe

BECOME A PATRON OF NIXES MATE.

For $50 receive two issues of *Nixes Mate Review*, plus our latest book, and a special literary treat.

For $100 receive two issues of *Nixes Mate Review*, plus our latest three books, and a special literary treat.

For $500 receive two issues of *Nixes Mate Review*, plus all the books in our catalog.

For $1000 receive all current and future issues of *Nixes Mate Review*, plus all the books in our catalog, all the available limited edition broadsides and chapbooks, various special literary treats, and all our future books.

Go to nixesmate.pub/patron

42° 19' 47.9" N · 70° 56' 43.9" W

Nixes Mate is a navigational hazard in Boston Harbor used during the colonial period to gibbet and hang pirates and mutineers.

Nixes Mate Books features small-batch artisanal literature, created by writers who use all 26 letters of the alphabet and then some, honing their craft the time-honored way: one line at a time.

nixesmate.pub